JB WIE

Jeffrey, Laura S.

Simon Wiesenthal :
  tracking down Nazi

Simon
Wiesenthal

People to Know

Simon Wiesenthal

Tracking Down Nazi Criminals

Laura S. Jeffrey

Enslow Publishers, Inc.

40 Industrial Road   PO Box 38
Box 398   Aldershot
Berkeley Heights, NJ 07922   Hants GU12 6BP
USA   UK

http://www.enslow.com

Library of Congress Cataloging-in-Publication Data

Jeffrey, Laura S.
   Simon Wiesenthal : tracking down Nazi criminals / Laura S.
Jeffrey.
      p.   cm. — (People to know)
   Includes bibliographical references and index.
   Summary: Presents the life and exploits of a Nazi-hunter,
including the stories of how he caught and brought to justice
such infamous war criminals as Adolf Eichmann.
   ISBN 0-89490-830-8
   1. Wiesenthal, Simon—Juvenile literature. 2. Holocaust
survivors—Biography—Juvenile literature. 3. Nazi hunters—
Biography—Juvenile literature. 4. War criminals—Germany—
Juvenile literature. 5. Holocaust, Jewish (1939–1945)—
Juvenile literature. [1. Wiesenthal, Simon. 2. Holocaust
survivors. 3. War criminals—Germany. 4. Holocaust, Jewish
(1939–1945)] I. Title. II. Series.
DS135.A93W5335 1997
940.53'18—dc21   97-8220
                                                      CIP
                                                    AC r97

Printed in the United States of America

10 9 8 7 6 5 4

Illustration Credits:
Courtesy of the Simon Wiesenthal Center Beit HaShoa Museum of Tolerance
Library/Archives, Los Angeles, CA, pp. 6, 15, 17, 22, 33, 37, 41, 43, 46, 50,
56, 59, 64, 68, 71; Courtesy of the Simon Wiesenthal Center Beit HaShoa
Museum of Tolerance, © Jim Mendenhall, pp. 10, 27, 76, 84, 88.

Cover Illustration:
Courtesy of the Simon Wiesenthal Center Beit HaShoa Museum of Tolerance
Library/Archives, Los Angeles, CA.

Contents

Simon Wiesenthal

And Justice for All

Los Angeles, California, is usually thought of as a glamorous, sometimes even frivolous, city, where television and film actors work and live. Yet close to the Los Angeles neighborhoods of Century City and Beverly Hills is a building that represents a solemn mission. At the Simon Wiesenthal Center, men and women make sure people all over the world remember the Holocaust. They also work to prevent such an enormous tragedy from occurring again.

The Holocaust was the murder of more than 6 million Jewish people in the years before and during World War II (1939–1945). The killings occurred throughout Europe, under the supervision of Adolf Hitler.

Hitler, who founded the Nazi political party, ruled Germany from 1933 until 1945. He dreamed of creating a "master race" of blond, blue-eyed Germans to rule the world.

Hitler was anti-Semitic. This means that he was prejudiced against Jewish people. As a minority, Jews have often been persecuted for their faith throughout history. In addition, when political or economic times were bad, people needed a scapegoat, and minority groups like the Jews were often blamed.[1]

In Germany, self-esteem had been extremely low since the country's defeat in World War I. In the 1930s the German economy collapsed. Hitler blamed the Jewish people for Germany's problems.[2] Anti-Semitism was not new in Germany, and Hitler's actions were tolerated and accepted by many of his countrymen.

As Hitler's army invaded countries throughout Europe, Hitler directed the Nazis to kill Jews. He also demanded the deaths of other people he considered to be enemies, including Catholics, Gypsies, Poles, and Slavs. By the time the United States and its allies finally defeated Germany in 1945, the Nazis had killed millions and millions of people.

Simon Wiesenthal, the man for whom the Los Angeles center is named, knows the horrors of the Holocaust firsthand. Along with other European Jews in the late 1930s, Wiesenthal had his rights as a citizen taken away. Then his home and property were confiscated. Finally, he was sent to the Nazi concentration camps, where conditions were brutal. When he was rescued by American soldiers in 1945, he was in very poor health. Yet he immediately began what became his life's work: finding the Nazis who had been responsible for such madness, and bringing them to justice.

Wiesenthal did not actually go out and arrest Nazis. Instead, he interviewed survivors and wrote detailed reports of Nazi atrocities. He also gathered information that pinpointed where many of the Nazis were hiding. Then he presented this information to the authorities.

Wiesenthal often had to struggle to be heard, because many government officials all over the world had little interest in prosecuting Nazis. His task became even more difficult as the years passed. For the public in general, World War II and the Nazi crimes became distant memories. But Wiesenthal would not, could not, forget. He pressed on. Largely because of his efforts, more than one thousand Nazis were located and brought to justice. These notorious criminals included Adolf Eichmann, who was the main person responsible for carrying out Hitler's orders to kill Jews. Karl Silberbauer, the Gestapo officer who arrested Anne Frank and her family, was also caught. The Gestapo was a secret police organization in Germany. Its members used very brutal tactics to gather information and find Jews.

Wiesenthal's long list of what he calls his "clients" even includes a woman, Hermine Braunsteiner. This cruel camp guard was found living in the United States, where she had become a naturalized citizen. If it had not been for Simon Wiesenthal, these people literally would have gotten away with murder.

Along the way, Wiesenthal wrote several books about his experiences. He opened the Los Angeles center in 1977. With its adjoining Museum of Tolerance, it became an international center for Holocaust remembrance, for the defense of human rights, and for Jewish people. One of its many achievements was producing *Genocide*, a 1981 documentary narrated by Elizabeth Taylor and the late Orson Welles. The film won an Academy Award. "I have received many honors in my lifetime," Wiesenthal said. "When I die, these honors will die with me. But the Simon Wiesenthal Center will live on as my legacy."[3]

At its Museum of Tolerance, the Simon Wiesenthal Center preserves and displays artifacts from the Holocaust. Shown here is the back view of the museum building.

Wiesenthal also served as a consultant for movies about World War II. He has won numerous honors and awards, but his success came with a price. For example, Wiesenthal's outspokenness often put him at odds not only with those prejudiced against him but also with other Jewish people. His life was threatened many times. Most important, he paid an enormous emotional price for his work. The Nazi hunter has never escaped the nightmare of the Holocaust.

"I'm doing this because I have to do it," Wiesenthal once said of his work. "I am not motivated by a sense of revenge. . . . I realized that *we must not forget.* If all of us forgot, the same thing might happen again, in twenty or fifty or a hundred years."[4]

World War II has been over for more than five decades. Those Nazis who managed to elude capture are old men by now, and many most likely are dead. In fact, the case of Erich Priebke was called the last Nazi war case.[5] Priebke, who had escaped to Argentina after the Germans were defeated, was finally arrested in November 1995 and returned to Italy. There he stood trial for the mass murder of more than three hundred Italians.

Yet Wiesenthal's work continues. He strives to educate people, particularly youths, about what happened, so that it will never happen again. Wiesenthal has said:

> *I am forever asking myself what I can do for those who have not survived. The answer I have found for myself . . . is: I want to be their mouthpiece, I want*

to keep their memory alive, to make sure the dead live on in that memory. But we, the survivors, have an obligation not only to the dead but also to future generations: we must pass on to them our experiences, so they can learn from them. Information is defense.

We are under an obligation to make young people realize how unique, how unbelievable, how exceptional the period of the Holocaust was. But by this very attempt, we make it difficult for them to accept our accounts as the truth and as facts. The incomprehensible remains incomprehensible.[6]

If Wiesenthal had not lived through it himself, perhaps he, too, would find the truth of the Holocaust difficult to believe. As a boy growing up in a European country that was called Austria-Hungary, young Simon certainly never could have envisioned this life for himself. Back in the days of his youth, before the Nazis rose to power and hate stormed his world, Wiesenthal had other goals. The young man wanted to be an architect.

As a Youth

New Year's Eve in 1908 was a particularly festive holiday for Hans Wiesenthal. Aside from celebrating the coming of a new year, the prosperous sugar trader and his wife, Rapp, were welcoming the birth of their first child. Simon Wiesenthal came into the world "about half an hour before the end of the year," as his mother later told him.[1] The child was born in his parents' home in Buchach, which was part of the empire known as Austria-Hungary.

Buchach was a town of about nine thousand people. Six thousand of them were Jewish. The Wiesenthals were very religious, and young Simon learned much about Judaism from his maternal grandmother. "All my education before school was my grandmother," he recalled years later, "with her stories of rabbis and miracles."[2]

As a young boy, Simon often visited his father's warehouse. He liked to build small houses out of the sugar cubes that were stored there. Perhaps it was then that his desire to become an architect first formed. His early childhood was happy—but too quickly, it came to an end. In 1914, when Simon was six years old, World War I began after the heir to the throne of the Austrian Empire, Archduke Francis Ferdinand, was assassinated. Fighting broke out and before long, several countries were involved. Austria-Hungary, Germany, and Turkey were on one side. France, the British Empire, Italy, and Russia were on the other.

Hans Wiesenthal was called to serve in the Austrian-Hungarian army. He died in battle in 1915. The Russians invaded Buchach, and Simon's town became a battleground. The Wiesenthals fled to Vienna, Austria. In that thriving city, Simon and his brother began school.

Meanwhile, the United States tried to remain neutral in World War I. It finally entered the war against Germany and its allies in April 1917, after American ships were repeatedly harassed in international waters by German submarines. That same year, the Russians left Buchach, and Simon and his family returned home. Tensions remained high, however, with Russian, Ukrainian, and Polish troops variously battling for control of the town.

Wiesenthal later recalled that regimes seemed to

Simon Wiesenthal spent most of his childhood in the town of Buchach, which had a large Jewish population.

change daily, and that his family often would get up not knowing who was in power on any particular day. In school, when Simon and the other students were asked to whom they swore their loyalty, Simon had to first check the picture on the wall of his classroom to learn who was his town's leader. One week it might be a Russian; the next, a Ukrainian; the week after that, a Pole.

No matter who was in power, Jews were always the target of animosity. Once, when Simon was ten, his mother sent him to a neighbor's house to borrow some yeast. A Ukrainian soldier saw him passing by.

Without provocation, he cut Simon's leg with his sword. The attack left a lifelong scar on the boy.

In 1918, a year after the United States entered the war, Germany and its allies were defeated. The Treaty of Versailles, signed in 1919, officially ended the war with Germany. This document required Germany to give up land, abolish much of its military, and pay extensive damages. The defeat left that country very poor for the next several years, and the German people grew dispirited.

In 1919, the Treaty of St. Germain officially ended the war with Austria-Hungary. Austria, Hungary, and Czechoslovakia became independent states. A part of the former empire was given to Poland, another new European nation.

It was in this atmosphere that Adolf Hitler, a politician who was twenty-five years old when World War I started, rose to leadership. In 1923, Hitler formed a new political party, the Nazis. (Nazi is short for the German words that mean National Socialist German Workers' party.) In 1925, Hitler's autobiography, *Mein Kampf* (German for "My Struggle"), was published. It contained his ideas for making Germany powerful and prosperous.

Germany, Hitler wrote, must be ruled by a *führer* ("leader") with absolute power. The führer and all his subordinates should be "pure" Germans. Germans were descendants of an ancient race called the Aryans, and Hitler believed this race to be superior to others. He believed that Aryans had weakened their race by marrying "inferior" people such as Jews.[3]

Hitler also wrote about an expanded Germany.

Simon Wiesenthal (center) was the leader of a troop of Boy Scouts in Buchach in 1923. All of these boys except one were killed in the Holocaust.

Because Austria, Hungary, and Poland, among other countries, had large German populations, the Nazi leader intended to take control of those lands.

Mein Kampf was a blueprint for what Hitler later came very close to accomplishing. But when the book was first published, few people paid much attention to it. Simon Wiesenthal certainly did not. He was busy preparing for his future. He attended the local high school, called Humanistic Gymnasium, in Buchach. It was there that he met Cyla Muller. Simon and his blond Jewish classmate began dating.

Simon's mother remarried in 1925 and moved with Simon's younger brother to Dolina, where her new husband owned a tile factory. Simon stayed behind in Buchach to finish school. He visited his family as often as he could. After he graduated from high school in 1928, he applied to Polytechnic Institute in Lvov, a major city in Austria-Hungary (now part of Ukraine.) The university limited the number of Jewish students it would accept, and Simon was denied admittance. Instead, he enrolled at Technical University of Prague and studied architecture and engineering.

Simon was popular with his fellow students. He had a good sense of humor and loved to tell funny tales. When he traveled home by train during school vacations, he liked to stay up all night entertaining the other passengers with his stories. By the time he arrived home, his voice was often very hoarse.

Simon received a degree in architectural engineering from the Technical University of Prague in 1932. He moved to Lvov and opened his own architecture firm. He began designing homes for wealthy people. "Right to the end, people surrounded themselves with possessions," Wiesenthal later said of the years leading to World War II. "They must have thought that somehow property would protect them. Maybe in those days, I thought that way, too."[4]

While Wiesenthal was practicing architecture, Hitler was growing more and more powerful. In 1933, Hitler became the leader of Germany. Three years later, Germany was sponsor of the 1936 Olympics. Hitler saw the Games as a perfect opportunity to prove to the world the superiority of his race. He had ruled that only Aryan athletes could compete for Germany.

Imagine Hitler's shock and anger when an African

American, Jesse Owens, won four gold medals in track and field events. In Hitler's eyes, blacks were an inferior race. Yet Owens had demonstrated that the Nazi leader's beliefs were wrong. Unfortunately, that did not make Hitler change his mind—or his evil plans.

A World in Turmoil

In 1936, after a long courtship interrupted by schooling and political turmoil, Simon Wiesenthal and Cyla Muller were married. Most newlyweds are optimistic that they will live happily ever after. Any similar thoughts that the Wiesenthals had would soon be erased. Hitler and the Nazis were now in power. The Wiesenthals' world—and the world of millions of other Jews across Europe—would never be the same again.

Hitler moved quickly to fulfill his promise to the German people to make their country a superpower. In August 1939, Germany and the Soviet Union signed a nonaggression pact. According to this agreement, neither country would interfere with the other's plans to invade Poland. So on September 1, the Germans invaded Poland from the west. Two weeks later, the Soviets invaded from the east. Britain and France, which had pledged to protect Poland, soon declared war on Germany and the Soviet Union. World War II had begun.

By mid-September, the Soviet army had taken over Wiesenthal's town of Lvov. Once again, Jews became targets. Prominent members of the Jewish community, including merchants, factory owners, doctors, lawyers, and teachers, were arrested. Wiesenthal's stepfather and brother were among those who were imprisoned. Wiesenthal's stepfather later died in prison, and his brother was shot to death by a Soviet soldier. Rapp Wiesenthal came to Lvov to live with her surviving son and daughter-in-law.

Those Jews who were not rounded up immediately were issued special passports that made them second-class citizens. They lost their jobs and the money in their bank accounts. A few months later, they were deported to Siberia. Most of them eventually died. Wiesenthal paid a bribe so that he, his wife, and mother were issued regular passports. Still, he was no longer permitted to practice architecture. Instead, Wiesenthal became a mechanic in a factory that produced bedsprings.

The Wiesenthals, along with other Jews, lived under strict rules. Their houses and businesses became the property of the government. They were not allowed to have overnight guests unless they first obtained permission. Also, shortages of food and

Simon Wiesenthal and his wife, Cyla.

clothing were frequent. Life was harsh, but it would become even worse.

In June 1941, less than two years after signing the nonaggression pact, Germany turned on the Soviet Union and invaded its territory. As Soviet troops retreated from Lvov, the Germans arrived. They celebrated their victory with a three-day pogrom, which is a massacre of Jews by the non-Jewish ruling class. Jewish men caught by the soldiers were hanged, shot, or beaten to death. Others were trampled to death or crushed beneath the wheels of cannons. When the pogrom was over, about six thousand Jews had been killed.

Wiesenthal managed to survive the pogrom by hiding in the cellar of a house. But in July 1941, a policeman broke into the house, arrested him, and took him to a prison. There, Wiesenthal and about one hundred other prominent Jews were ordered to line up in several rows facing the wall. Then, the killings began. One by one, the prisoners were being shot and carried out to be buried.

Shortly before it was Wiesenthal's turn to be killed, church bells rang. The executioners decided to take a break from the murders so they could attend services. Wiesenthal and about twenty other survivors were granted a temporary reprieve and were taken to prison cells.

During the night, a policeman working for the Nazis came to Wiesenthal's cell. The policeman had once worked as a carpenter for Wiesenthal. "I've got to get you out of here," the man whispered. "You know what they'll do tomorrow morning."[1]

The policeman told his supervisors that Wiesenthal was a spy who needed to be taken away for questioning. Wiesenthal escaped and returned home. A few days later, he and other healthy men were rounded up for work assignments. Wiesenthal's life had been spared, but things certainly were not easy for him. Every day, he and the others worked long, grueling hours. Then they returned home to a part of the city that had been fenced off and turned into a ghetto where all Jewish people were ordered to live.

In October 1941, Simon and Cyla Wiesenthal were ordered to report to the Janowska concentration camp near Lvov. Wiesenthal's mother remained in the ghetto. A concentration camp is a place where people are held against their will, without benefit of legal proceedings. The first Nazi concentration camps had been organized shortly after Hitler came to power in 1933. At first, they were set up to intimidate people, mainly Jews. However, many of the camps were later turned into killing camps, or extermination camps, so that Hitler could more efficiently get rid of Jewish people.

The days at Janowska were extremely difficult. The prisoners there spent long, hard hours cutting stone and digging burial pits. They were not given much food to eat.

A few months later, the Wiesenthals were transferred again. This time, they were sent to a forced labor camp serving the repair shop for Lvov's Eastern Railroad. Cyla polished brass and nickel pieces, while Simon painted swastikas, the Nazi symbol, on captured Polish locomotives. Wiesenthal later called the camp "an island of sanity in a sea of madness."[2]

"My boss was Heinrich Guenthert . . . a good guy," and secretly anti-Nazi, he said. "One cold day he saw me painting a sign freehandedly and asked me what schooling I had. As an architect, I had studied art, but I didn't want to tell him. Jewish intellectuals were being killed. So I told him I had gone to a . . . handicraft school."[3]

Another worker, who was perhaps trying to prove his loyalty to Guenthert, revealed Wiesenthal's true background. "Why did you lie to me?" Guenthert asked Wiesenthal. "You know a false answer can bring the Gestapo [Germany's dreaded secret police]. Now, I'm an engineer myself. No more freezing your hands out here. You come to the office."[4]

In his new job as a draftsman, Wiesenthal had a little freedom and comfort. He was able to make contact with the Polish underground, citizens who were working secretly to sabotage the Germans. The underground wanted information about the rail lines, so they would know where to plant bombs to disrupt service. Wiesenthal said he would give them this information in exchange for a false passport for Cyla. Wiesenthal was desperate for her to escape. He believed that with her blond hair, she could pass as a Gentile, or non-Jewish person. Cyla Wiesenthal was provided with a false passport and spirited out of the camp in the fall of 1942.

That year was even more brutal for Jews, as the Nazis formally began the Final Solution. This was Hitler's plan to systematically kill Jews and other non-Aryans. He and his fellow Nazis accomplished this with elaborate planning. Their victims were herded onto trains and sent to concentration camps. There, they were gassed, shot, or tortured to death.

From the railyard, Wiesenthal watched as thousands of Jews were forced aboard trains that were bound for the camps. In August, a few months before his wife escaped, Wiesenthal noticed elderly women being herded aboard train cars that were already overflowing with people. The cars sat under the burning sun for three days while the women screamed for water. Wiesenthal later learned that his mother had been aboard one of those train cars. She died in the Belzec concentration camp.

Wiesenthal himself had another very close brush with death in April 1943. In celebration of Hitler's birthday, the Nazis running the railyard decided to shoot some Jews. Wiesenthal and the other chosen men and women were ordered to strip off their clothes and line up. As the shooting began, Wiesenthal closed his eyes. Suddenly, he heard his name being called. Someone was needed to paint a giant "Happy Birthday" poster for Hitler. On Guenthert's orders, a guard chose Wiesenthal for the chore. "For a long time," Wiesenthal recalled later, "I was the only person I knew in the camps who still believed in miracles."[5]

Another day, Wiesenthal and some other prisoners were sent to a makeshift hospital to help with cleanup. While they were there, a nurse approached Wiesenthal and asked him to come with her. She led him to a bed where a heavily bandaged German

The Simon Wiesenthal Center displays clothing and other reminders of the concentration camps of the Holocaust.

soldier lay. The soldier had asked the nurse to find him a Jew. He wanted to make a confession.

"I know that at this moment thousands of men are dying," the soldier whispered. "It is neither infrequent nor extraordinary. I am resigned to dying soon, but before that I want to talk about an experience which is torturing me. Otherwise I cannot die in peace."[6]

The soldier went on to describe how he had participated in the killing of three hundred Jewish civilians in one village. Many of the dead were women and children. The soldier had been shot in a subsequent battle. Now, facing his own death, he sought relief from his painful memories. He asked Wiesenthal to forgive him:

> *I know that what I have told you is terrible. In the long nights while I have been waiting for death, time and time again I have longed to talk about it to a Jew and beg forgiveness from him. Only I didn't know whether there were any Jews left. . . . I know that what I am asking is almost too much for you, but without your answer I cannot die in peace.*[7]

Wiesenthal did not reply. Instead, he left the room without saying a word. Later, his actions would haunt him. He wrote about this experience in *The Sunflower,* a book that was published in 1976.

In the spring of 1943, Wiesenthal made plans to escape from the camp. Guenthert had been allowing Wiesenthal, accompanied by a guard, to shop for supplies in a nearby town. One day, while the guard waited outside, his Jewish prisoner simply walked in the front door of a store and then sneaked out the back entrance. Wiesenthal managed to get in touch with the Polish underground and was hidden in the attics or under the floorboards of various homes. During this time, he gave the underground workers technical advice on how to build bunkers and lines of fortification. Back at the labor camp, most of the prisoners were soon killed as part of the Final Solution.

Wiesenthal experienced eight months of "freedom." It came to an end one day in June 1944. A Polish police officer working for the Nazis was undoubtedly tipped off by someone. He broke into the house where Wiesenthal was hiding, found him under the floorboards, and arrested him. Wiesenthal was returned to the Janowska concentration camp.

It seemed certain that Wiesenthal's time to die had finally come. He had been keeping a diary of his experiences, and it had been confiscated. Sure enough, two days after Wiesenthal arrived at the camp, a truck with two Gestapo agents came to pick him up for questioning. One of the agents had the reputation of being very sadistic. "I knew I was finished," Wiesenthal recalled. "The only question was how he would finish me. I didn't want to know the answer."[8]

After Wiesenthal climbed onto the truck, he tried to commit suicide. He cut his wrists with a razor blade he had concealed in his shirt cuff. The Nazis took him to a prison hospital in Lvov. They wanted him well so that they would be able to question him. Once again, Wiesenthal had escaped death. How long would his luck hold?

Final Days As a Prisoner

Timing was once again on Simon Wiesenthal's side after his suicide attempt. On June 6, 1944, troops from the United States, Britain, and other countries invaded Normandy, France, which was under German control. The goal was to liberate that country, and eventually all of Europe, from the Nazis. This day is now known as D-Day.

"The best part of the invasion is that I have the feeling that friends are approaching," Anne Frank wrote in her diary shortly after D-Day. Anne, a Jewish girl hiding from the Nazis with her family, continued: "We have been oppressed by those terrible Germans for so long, they have had their knives so at our throats, that the thought of friends and delivery fills us with confidence! Now it doesn't concern the Jews any more; no, it concerns Holland and all occupied Europe. Perhaps, Margot [her sister] says, I may yet be able to go back to school in September or October."[1]

•   •   •   •   •

The United States had entered World War II in December 1941, after Japan bombed the American military base at Pearl Harbor, Hawaii. United States government and military leaders had long suspected the Japanese were planning some sort of attack. However, they were caught completely off guard. As a result, the base was devastated. As Japanese planes dropped their bombs, American fighter planes were unable to get off the ground to counterattack. Sailors aboard docked ships were trapped, unable to defend themselves. The Japanese sank or badly damaged eight battleships and ten other American ships. Almost two hundred American planes were destroyed, and several others were damaged. About twenty-four hundred United States military personnel and seventy civilians were killed. It was a total victory for the Japanese.

Shortly after the attack, Germany declared war on the United States. Things looked very grim for the Americans as the Japanese continued their assaults during the next days and weeks. They captured Guam, Wake Island, and the Philippines.

By early 1942, however, Americans had rallied. A spirit of national unity, summed up by the slogan "Remember Pearl Harbor," took over.[2] Thousands and thousands of American men of all ages volunteered for military duty or were drafted. Women went to work in American factories, turning out supplies and weapons for the troops. American President Franklin Roosevelt declared that the United States would fight alongside Great Britain and the Soviet Union until the Axis forces—Germany, Japan, and Italy—unconditionally surrendered.

The Allied forces decided on a "Europe First" strategy. This meant that they would focus on defeating Hitler in Europe. After that was accomplished, they would focus on defeating Japan. Fierce battles occurred at sea and in the air. With the Normandy invasion in 1944, ground battles intensified. This time, the Allied troops were victorious. In three months, they liberated the French capital of Paris.

Two months later, most of the German troops had retreated from France, Luxemburg, Belgium, and parts of Holland. With total defeat imminent, German troops all over Europe began retreating toward their home country. They abandoned their units and refused to fight. Though Adolf Hitler vowed to continue the war, many of his troops realized that it was a lost cause.

By July 1944, Allied troops were moving closer to Lvov, where Wiesenthal was still in the prison hospital after his suicide attempt. He knew he was soon to be questioned—and almost certainly killed. Suddenly an Allied plane dropped a bomb near the hospital. In the confusion, Wiesenthal ran over to a group of Jews who were being loaded onto a truck bound for the Janowska concentration camp.

Once they arrived at the camp, most of the Jews were shot. However, Wiesenthal and thirty-three other prisoners were randomly chosen to live. They were told that they were going to leave with their guards. Then they were marched out of town. The Nazi soldiers did this because if they had prisoners to guard, they would not have to face an almost certain death on the battlefield.

The Nazi guards and the Jewish prisoners spent the next several months marching from concentration camp to concentration camp, making their way westward and dodging the Allied troops. One afternoon, a Nazi guard named Merz told Wiesenthal to

The entrance to the Janowska concentration camp. Simon Wiesenthal knew firsthand the horrors of this camp. He narrowly escaped death there more than once.

accompany him to a nearby village, where they would search for food.

It was a hot day, and the two men decided to rest for a while in a forest. Merz had been one of a few Nazis who had not been cruel, Wiesenthal recalled later. "He'd never beaten anyone, never shouted at us. . . . Still I was not prepared for what was to come."[3]

> *Merz said to me . . . "Suppose an eagle took you to America, Wiesenthal. . . . What would you tell them? . . . Just imagine, Wiesenthal, that you were arriving in New York, and the people asked you, 'How was it in those German concentration camps? What did they do to you?'"*[4]

Wiesenthal hesitated, then replied that he would tell the truth about what had happened.

"Yes. I've thought about it, many times," Merz replied. "I've seen what has happened to your people. I'm [a Nazi], but sometimes I wake up in the middle of the night, and I don't know whether it's a dream or the truth."[5]

Then Merz said something Wiesenthal would never forget:

> *You would tell the truth to the people in America. That's right. And you know what would happen, Wiesenthal? They wouldn't believe you. They'd say you were crazy. Might even put you away. How can anyone believe this terrible business—unless he has lived through it?*[6]

In February 1945, the ragtag group finally arrived at Mauthausen concentration camp in Austria. Wiesenthal was one of the few prisoners who had managed to survive the ordeal, but he was very weak. In the next few months, he grew even sicker. His weight dropped to less than one hundred pounds, and he spent most of his days lying in a bunk. During his journey to the camp, he had met a group of prisoners who were also on the move. Someone in the group told Wiesenthal that his beloved wife, Cyla, had been killed when a Nazi bombed the house she was hiding out in.

Wiesenthal seemingly had no reason to live. Later, he would attribute his survival to a Polish guard who took an interest in him. The guard sometimes brought Wiesenthal bits of food. The prisoner and his captor also talked about what they were going to do when the war was over. They believed the fighting would be over soon because they could hear Allied planes flying overhead.

The guard said he wanted to return to Poland and open a coffee house. Since Wiesenthal was an architect, the guard said, would he draw the plans?

The guard brought Wiesenthal paper and pencils, and the former architect began to draw. Wiesenthal later said that the activity helped him forget where he was and what had happened to him, his family, his people. He made detailed drawings for the coffee house and even designed uniforms for the waiters. Wiesenthal and the guard had long talks about the colors of the rugs and the shape of the tables.

Meanwhile, the war was indeed coming to an end. By the spring of 1945, German forces in Italy had surrendered. On April 12, the United States announced that President Roosevelt had died. He was succeeded in office by his relatively unknown vice president, Harry Truman.

Hitler believed that Roosevelt's death would stall the Allies, and that the Nazis could emerge victorious. He ordered his men to continue fighting; anyone who disobeyed him would be shot or hanged immediately.

The Nazis, however, paid little attention to their once beloved leader. Hitler himself finally saw that defeat was inevitable. He killed himself on April 30, 1945.

As the Allied troops entered Germany, the atrocities of the Holocaust were finally revealed. American soldiers liberated the concentration camp at Buchenwald on April 11 and the camp at Dachau on April 19. They were horrified and sickened by what they saw. Bodies of Jewish prisoners were piled up three or four high, waiting to be burned or buried. The few surviving prisoners were starving and very weak.

American soldiers ordered German townfolk to tour the camps so that they could see for themselves what had occurred. Many civilians denied knowing that Jews had been tortured and killed in the camps, which were so close to their own homes.

On the morning of May 5, 1945, American troops arrived at Mauthausen. Wiesenthal slowly made his way outside, where he saw a tank flying an American flag. "Every star [on the flag] was a star of hope," Wiesenthal said. "I . . . wanted to touch one of those stars."[7] He struggled toward the tank but fainted. An American soldier picked him up and returned him to his bunk.

Two days after Mauthausen was liberated, Germany unconditionally surrendered, and the war in Europe ended. The Allies then turned their attention to defeating the final Axis power, Japan. Fighting had been particularly bloody, but the Japanese had vowed to continue the war. The Allies felt they needed to do something drastic. On August 6, 1945, an American B-29 bomber dropped an atomic bomb on the Japanese city of Hiroshima. Three days later, a second bomb was dropped, this time on the city of Nagasaki. With thousands dead and destruction almost total, Japan finally surrendered.

Simon Wiesenthal and others gathered on May 5, 1946, to commemorate the one-year anniversary of the liberation of the Mauthausen concentration camp.

On September 2, 1945, Japanese and American military leaders met aboard the U.S. battleship *Missouri* so that the Japanese could sign the surrender documents. General Douglas MacArthur declared:

> *It is my earnest hope and indeed the hope of all mankind that from this solemn occasion a better world shall emerge out of the blood and carnage of the past—a world founded upon faith and understanding—a world dedicated to the dignity of man and the fulfillment of his most cherished wish—for freedom, tolerance and justice.*[8]

World War II was officially over. Many people were anxious to forget the horrors of war and look to the future. Simon Wiesenthal could not do that. He had lived while so many had died. He could not abandon his fellow Jews, those millions who had not survived.

The First Client

Many of the Holocaust survivers became known as "displaced persons." They had no homes to return to or were too weak and malnourished to leave the camps. The concentration camps took on a new role as "displaced persons camps." After Mauthausen was liberated, Simon Wiesenthal was one of the many former prisoners who stayed to recuperate. The Americans also stayed. They nursed the freed men and women back to health and helped them reestablish their lives.

One day, without provocation, Wiesenthal was beaten by another former prisoner, who was a Gentile. To Wiesenthal, this beating was worse than anything that had already happened to him. "Now the war is over," he thought, "and the Jews are still being beaten."[1] Encouraged by the other Jews at the camp, Wiesenthal decided to complain to the American officer in charge, Colonel Richard Seibel.

Still weak, Wiesenthal had to be helped by two others as he made his way to the colonel's office. When Seibel heard what had happened, he ordered the other prisoner to be brought to his office to apologize to Wiesenthal.

While Wiesenthal was meeting with Seibel, he noticed an office marked "War Crimes." Nazis were being taken in there to be questioned by the Americans. Many of the Nazis were so scared that they were shaking. They also were denying their involvement in the atrocities. Wiesenthal, who had spent so many years fearing these people, was amazed. He recalled:

> *For the first time in my life, I saw what enormous cowards these people were; how, instead of dealing with their guilt, they tried to deny it . . . [I] realized one thing: the Germans . . . would not simply acknowledge with shame what we had experienced—they would dispute it. Every one of us survivors was a witness and had the duty to bear witness. Most of all a surviving Jew. The realization that I had remained alive while so many others—better ones, cleverer ones, more decent ones—had died, at some moments almost seemed to me an offense against justice. I could restore the balance only by ensuring that the dead received justice.[2]*

Wiesenthal asked the Americans if he could work for the United States War Crimes Unit. The Americans could not understand why he would choose to stay.

After the war, Simon Wiesenthal began his work to educate people about the Holocaust so that it would never happen again. "We, the survivors, have an obligation not only to the dead but also to future generations," he said.

Why not return home and design houses? they asked. Wiesenthal replied that he did not want to do that.

"For all I knew I was one of the few thousand Jews surviving in Europe," he recalled later. "My wife. . . . I thought she was dead. The buildings I had built . . . were erased. My parents were dead. I could not go back. . . . To go on living was a burden, but someone had to live on and tell what it was really like."[3]

After he insisted, Wiesenthal was told to write a letter explaining everything he had witnessed and who was responsible. The former prisoner spent three days working on the document. It was so detailed that the Americans eagerly accepted his help. Wiesenthal began working for the War Crimes Unit.

The former prisoner's first assignment was to arrest an SS officer. The SS was an elite group of Nazi combat troops that supervised the concentration camps. The SS officer lived on the third floor of an apartment house. Wiesenthal was still so weak that the man he arrested had to help him down the stairs.[4]

During the next several months, Wiesenthal interviewed his fellow survivors. The testimonies he gathered were later used in war crimes trials held by the United States military. He also worked at the newly established Jewish Committee in Linz, Austria. This group helped survivors get in touch with family members. The task was very slow, since mail and telephone services were restricted.

Late in 1945, Wiesenthal received some wonderful news: His wife was alive! One night, after going over a list of survivors, Wiesenthal had come across the name of a high-school classmate. He wrote a letter to his friend. Coincidentally, the day after receiving the letter, the friend received a visit from Cyla. She had managed to escape from the bombed house. Still passing as a Gentile, Cyla had been sent to work in a German machine-gun factory. She was told that her husband had killed himself during the war.

With their friend's help, Simon and Cyla were able to get in touch with each other. They were finally reunited at the end of 1945. Together, they had lost ninety family members in the Holocaust. At least they finally had each other again. The next year, 1946, their daughter, Pauline Rosa, was born. As Wiesenthal said later, "Nobody has ever wanted a baby as much as we did."[5]

After the war, Simon Wiesenthal (second from left) and his wife, Cyla, celebrated with friends.

6

Gathering Evidence

In 1946, the Allied forces set up a court in Nuremberg, Germany, to prosecute Nazi officials for war crimes. Twenty-two of Hitler's men were tried, including Hermann Goering. He was a close friend of Adolf Hitler's who had been in charge of the German air force. Many of the accused argued that they were merely carrying out the orders of their superiors, but this defense was rejected. The court found the German government and its soldiers guilty of war crimes "on a vast scale, never before seen in the history of war, attended by every conceivable circumstance of cruelty and horror."[1] The Nazis had been responsible for the deaths of about 6 million Jews and 5 million other people. About 40 million others in the world had been killed in the fighting and bombings during World War II.

In the Nuremberg Trials, as the prosecutions came to be called, Goering and eleven others were sentenced to death. Goering killed himself before he could be executed. In fact, many of the highest-ranked Nazis, including Adolf Hitler, Joseph Goebbels, and Heinrich Himmler, committed suicide before they were even brought to trial. Hundreds of other Nazis managed to escape to other countries and resume their lives under assumed identities.

Meanwhile, the victory of 1945 did not bring long-lasting peace in Europe. After the war, the Allies divided among themselves some of the countries that had been under enemy control. For example, Germany was divided into zones of occupation. These zones were supervised by British, American, French, and Soviet troops. The Soviets controlled the eastern zones, while the other troops controlled the western zone.

In 1949, Germany was permanently divided into two separate states. The Federal Republic of Germany, a democracy, was established in the western part of the country. The Democratic Republic of Germany, which was communist, was set up in the eastern part. The Democratic Republic of Germany imposed strict censorship on its citizens and placed armed guards at its border to prevent people from escaping. (The two Germanys were reunited in 1985.)

Other countries were also divided after the war. Many of these divisions were supposed to be temporary. However, the Soviet occupation of

Jewish survivors mourn friends and family at a memorial to victims of the Holocaust in the Jewish cemetery in Buchach.

countries in Eastern Europe soon caused concern in the United States and other Western countries. A fear grew that the Soviets would seize this volatile time as an opportunity to gain worldwide power for communism, their system of government.

The Nazis had been defeated, but now the Americans believed there was a new threat to world peace: the Soviets. This was the beginning of the Cold War, a term that described tension, but not actual combat, between the United States and the Soviet Union.

As attention turned toward the Soviet threat, the capture of the Nazis who had escaped punishment became less of a priority to the Americans. Wiesenthal vowed to continue the job on his own. In 1947, he opened the Jewish Documentation Center in Linz, Austria. He was aided by about thirty volunteers and part-time staff members. "I am no longer working for the Americans," he told them. "Life is too simple for them. They think that in America they have cowboys and Indians and in Europe we have Nazis and Jews. I feel it is our duty to do this job with our own hands."[2]

The center was a lean operation. There were no big salaries, fancy offices, or special perks. Every day, Wiesenthal and his workers visited the displaced-persons camps set up for Holocaust survivors who had nowhere else to go. They interviewed the survivors about their experiences, carefully recording names, dates, and geographic locations. Wiesenthal would not accept hearsay, which is something that a person has heard but does not actually know to be true. The reports had to contain only the information that came from survivors' firsthand knowledge.

Wiesenthal also organized card files. One file listed locations where Nazi brutalities had occurred. Another held the names of Nazis and their crimes. Eventually, this list grew to more than twenty thousand names. Still another file listed witnesses to the horrors.

The center's first big catch came in September 1947. Late one night, Wiesenthal was visited at home by two men living in an Austrian displaced-persons camp. They told Wiesenthal that they had just heard that a rich farmer living near their camp was known for hating Jews. They figured he must be Adolf

Eichmann. Eichmann was the chief of the Gestapo's Jewish department. He had supervised the implementation of the Final Solution.

The next morning, Wiesenthal drove to the farmer's village and stopped at the local police station. He asked the commander there about the big farm on the hill. The commander told him that it belonged to a man named Franz Murer. The farmer was not the dreaded Eichmann, but he was a wanted criminal. Murer's nickname was "the butcher of Wilna." He had been responsible for the killings of almost eighty thousand Jews in that Lithuanian town. After the war, he had simply returned to his family farm.

Wiesenthal quickly left the police station, then drove to the camp. Over a loudspeaker, he asked whether anyone there had any firsthand knowledge of Franz Murer. Seven people came forward, and Wiesenthal took their statements. He then returned to the police station and handed over the statements. Murer was arrested and eventually turned over to the Soviets, since his crimes had been committed in an area that was now under Soviet control. Murer was found guilty and sentenced to serve twenty-five years of hard labor.

Later, Wiesenthal learned that the Soviets had released Murer after seven years. He had returned to his beloved farm. Wiesenthal gathered more evidence against Murer and submitted it to the government of Austria. The Nazi was arrested again and charged with other counts of murder. At the trial, the new testimony included that of a father whose teenage son had been shot before his eyes. Another person testified that Murer had shot her sister after the sister took a piece of bread from another woman. Then, in a rage, Murer had shot four other people who happened to be nearby. Despite such strong assertions, an Austrian jury found Murer not guilty. He returned to his farm.

Murer had been easy to find. Tracking down other Nazis would prove to be more difficult. Many of the most powerful of Hitler's men had formed a secret organization called Odessa. Toward the end of the war, when defeat was imminent, they had hidden away money, created papers for themselves with false identities, and planned escape routes to countries where they would be safe from prosecution. After World War II was over, they seemed to have vanished.

Wiesenthal found much support among the Jewish community for his efforts. Some people, however, believed that more needed to be done. After all, the courts handed down light sentences to some of the Nazis, or juries had found them not guilty despite overwhelming evidence. One visitor to Wiesenthal's office said he represented a group that wanted access to his files on the Nazis, "so that we can exterminate them as they exterminated us."[3]

"No, no," Wiesenthal replied. "We will not be like them. We will use the law. If you kill them, the world will never learn what they did. There must be an accounting. There must be testimony in court, a record for history."[4]

Yet Wiesenthal himself admitted that his task was emotionally very difficult. "I drag around with me not

After the war ended, synagogues were established for Holocaust survivors. Simon Wiesenthal is shown here in the first Displaced Person's Synagogue in 1946.

only the memory of what I experienced, but also the sufferings of so many witnesses who have told me their stories," he once said. "Sometimes the borderlines get blurred, then I find it difficult to differentiate between what I and the other person experienced."[5]

In December 1948, a year after Wiesenthal's big catch, world tensions erupted again. The Soviets reported that their troops had left North Korea, which wanted to remain a communist nation. However, the United Nations was not allowed to visit North Korea to verify this. The following June, United States troops left South Korea, which wanted to remain democratic.

A year later, in June 1950, the North Korean army invaded South Korea. Eventually, troops from the United States as well as Great Britain, Canada, France, Greece, and other countries came to the South Koreans' aid.

With the United States and others mired in another war, interest in the Nazi issue came to a standstill. Wiesenthal had thousands of reports, but no government seemed interested in pursuing or prosecuting the war criminals. Wiesenthal insisted:

> *I am right when I protest against the cover-up and the forgetting of Nazi crimes. Their stories must be told and heard. They should be written down and read, so that others, born later, can learn from it. Their [the Holocaust survivors'] suffering gives me the strength to do the right thing, and may help others recognize that this barbarity, this Nazi tyranny, can never be repeated.*[6]

Wiesenthal's pleas went unheard. Frustrated, he

closed his center in 1954. He sent most of his files to a documentation center in Israel. This republic in the Middle East had been proclaimed a homeland for Jews in 1948.

There was one file that Wiesenthal held on to, that of Adolf Eichmann. In the years since his search had yielded Murer, he had gathered many more clues about Hitler's evil right-hand man. Wiesenthal grew more and more determined to find him.

Tracking Adolf Eichmann

After Simon Wiesenthal closed the Jewish Documentation Center, he spent most of his time helping fellow survivors put their lives back in order. He became a welfare officer in Austria for a Jewish relief organization. Later, he directed occupational training schools.

While Wiesenthal was not officially hunting Nazis, the case of Adolf Eichmann continued to haunt him. Wiesenthal had first heard of this Nazi in 1945, when he was working for the United States War Crimes Unit. At first Wiesenthal was not too interested in pursuing Eichmann; he was more concerned with finding the people responsible for the atrocities he had personally witnessed. Yet as he read information that the Americans had already compiled and heard other stories from survivors, Wiesenthal built resolve: Eichmann must be caught. He had been a top executive in the business of killing Jews.

Back in the summer of 1945, Wiesenthal had learned from his own landlady that Eichmann's parents lived in Linz, four houses down from where Wiesenthal was staying. Wiesenthal had given this tip to the Americans in the war crimes office. They searched the Eichmanns' house, but nothing that could be tied to their son Adolf was found. In fact, no personal items of Adolf Eichmann's seemed to exist. He had destroyed everything before Germany's defeat.

In August 1945, Wiesenthal had also heard a rumor that Eichmann was hiding in an Austrian village called Altaussee. An American investigator went there. He found a woman named Veronika Liebl and her three children. Liebl said she had been Eichmann's wife, but they were now divorced. Liebl also said she had not seen her former husband since two months before the war ended and that she did not have any photographs of him. Wiesenthal doubted that the Eichmanns had divorced; Liebl had reportedly acted suspiciously.

Wiesenthal later learned that Eichmann had been captured and sent to an American prison camp shortly after the war ended. The Americans knew he was a Nazi, but they did not realize how instrumental he had been in the devious plans. Eichmann was assigned to work on a construction crew in a nearby town. One day in June 1945, Eichmann went to work with the crew and never returned to the camp. He would later hide in Germany and Austria for four years before making his way to a monastery in Italy. Eichmann always seemed to be one step ahead of his pursuers.

After Liebl and her children were found, Wiesenthal was approached by some Jews. They wanted to kidnap Eichmann's children and announce that they would be killed unless their father turned himself in. Wiesenthal later said:

> *I had many arguments against their plan, but only one convinced them. A man who unemotionally ordered the death of one million children would show no emotion for his own children. Even if he were deeply hurt by their plan, he would not save [them] by giving himself up. He is not that kind of man.*[1]

In 1947, Wiesenthal found a former mistress of Eichmann's. She had a photo of the Nazi! It was more than a decade old, but it was all Wiesenthal had to identify Eichmann. Wiesenthal made several copies to distribute on "wanted" posters.

The next year, in 1948, Wiesenthal learned that Liebl had petitioned the courts to declare her supposed ex-husband dead. To support her claim, she presented testimony from the Czechoslovakian minister of agriculture. He said he had seen Eichmann dead on April 30, 1945, in Prague.

"I was sure that Eichmann had plotted this move," Wiesenthal recalled. "If he were declared legally dead, all governments would quit their search for him and he would be free."[2]

Wiesenthal and his team decided to investigate.

Wiesenthal spent many years in pursuit of the dreaded Nazi commander Adolf Eichmann.

They quickly learned that the agriculture minister was married to Liebl's sister. They also produced evidence that Eichmann had been in the American camp in June 1945, two months after the official had supposedly seen him dead. The court disallowed the claim, and the search for Eichmann continued.

In 1952, Veronika Liebl and her three children disappeared. Wiesenthal felt certain that she had joined her husband. But where? It was a question that Wiesenthal would mull over for years, even after he closed his documentation center in 1954.

Wiesenthal became so caught up in the Eichmann case that it began to affect his health. He became ill and had trouble sleeping. He visited a doctor for help and was told, "I can't do anything for you. You need a distraction from your work. A hobby."[3]

Wiesenthal decided to take up stamp collecting. It would prove to be a smart choice. One day in 1953, Wiesenthal was discussing stamps with another collector. This collector mentioned that he had recently received a letter from a friend living in Argentina. The collector showed Wiesenthal the beautiful stamp, then began reading the letter. It contained two sentences that made Wiesenthal jump: "This awful swine Eichmann who ordered the Jews about. He lives near Buenos Aires . . ."[4]

Finally, Wiesenthal had a solid lead on Eichmann's whereabouts. The next day, Wiesenthal sent this information along with the old photo of Eichmann to the World Jewish Congress in New York and the Israeli consulate in Vienna. However, the United States Federal Bureau of Investigation had received information that Eichmann was in Syria. It took several years for the authorities to track down these leads. In the meantime, Wiesenthal learned that Liebl and Eichmann had never divorced.

In 1959, the Israeli government contacted Wiesenthal. They told him that they had found Mrs. Eichmann and her children living with a German named Ricardo Klement in Buenos Aires. Wiesenthal was certain that Klement was in fact Adolf Eichmann. "We must be certain," the Israelis told him. "We can't make a mistake in identification."[5]

Wiesenthal was asked if he could somehow obtain a more recent photo of Eichmann. The photo that Wiesenthal had originally given the Israelis was now twenty-five years old. A few months later, Eichmann's father died. As Wiesenthal read the obituary in the newspaper, he remembered that Eichmann had four brothers. One of them, Otto, was said to look very much like Adolf. Wiesenthal hired two photographers to hide in the cemetery during the funeral and take pictures of Otto and the other brothers. Then he had the photographs enlarged.

Wiesenthal met with the Israelis and showed them the photos. "Let your imagination age Eichmann in accordance with the way his brothers look today, especially . . . Otto," he told them. "What you see in your mind's eye is probably a very good likeness of this Ricardo Klement."[6]

In May 1960, three months after the funeral of Eichmann's father, Wiesenthal received a telegram from Israel's Holocaust center. Klement was indeed

Simon Wiesenthal and his daughter, Pauline, visited Mauthausen in 1961.

Adolf Eichmann, and the Israelis had captured him in Buenos Aires. "Congratulations on your excellent work," the telegram said.[7]

Eichmann was taken to Israel, where he was charged with mass murder. Wiesenthal first laid eyes on the Nazi at his trial. He was surprised at Eichmann's appearance. Instead of a scary monster, Eichmann resembled "a bookkeeper who is afraid to ask for a raise," Wiesenthal thought.[8]

Adolf Eichmann was found guilty and was sentenced to death. In May 1961, sixteen years after the end of World War II, Eichmann was hanged in Israel.

Seeing justice served gave Wiesenthal a great sense of satisfaction. Later, he said:

> *Until the trial there were millions of people in Germany and in Austria who pretended not to know or didn't want to know about the enormity of the SS crimes. The trial did away with such self-deception; after it, no one could claim ignorance.*[9]

In the years ahead, the Eichmann capture would be called Simon Wiesenthal's "greatest coup."[10] It would not be his only one, however. Confident that support was finally on the side of the survivors, Wiesenthal decided it was time to reopen the Jewish Documentation Center.

8

Case Files

Simon Wiesenthal reopened the Jewish Documentation Center in November 1961, this time in Vienna, Austria. In the years since then, he has worked to bring more than one thousand Nazis to prosecution. In his modest office, with only a secretary helping him, Wiesenthal pored over official documents, newspaper clippings, letters, and tips called or written in from people around the world.

Wiesenthal rarely traveled outside Germany and Austria. Instead, he relied on a network of volunteers who offered clues and assistance. Information came not only from Holocaust survivors but also from former Nazis. Perhaps out of a sense of guilt, perhaps angry that some of those most responsible for the crimes had escaped punishment, they often gave Wiesenthal valuable insights. He also worked in close contact with war crimes investigators in Israel and, later, the United States.

Wiesenthal's office was filled with newspapers. On one wall was a huge map. It pinpointed Nazi death camps and the number of people who died in each one. Other walls featured awards and certificates that Wiesenthal had received from around the world.[1]

Wiesenthal had some firm rules on how to proceed with cases. He insisted on quiet, careful investigation. He did not seek or accept publicity until the case had been completely prepared. Wiesenthal also focused not on revenge, but rather on the education of future generations.

"The schools would fail through their silence, the church through its forgiveness and the home through the denials or the silence of the parents," he once said. "The new generation has to hear what the older generation refuses to tell it."[2]

Wiesenthal scored many victories. For example, he identified the Gestapo agent who arrested Anne Frank and her family. Anne was a Jewish teenager who lived in the Netherlands. During World War II, she spent two years hiding in the attic of a house in Amsterdam with her family. The Franks were discovered and arrested in 1944. Anne died of typhoid in the Bergen-Belsen concentration camp in March 1945, two months before Germany surrendered.

Anne had kept a diary during her years in hiding. It had been overlooked when the Nazis raided the house. Her father, the only surviving family member, found it after the war. It was published in 1947 as *The Diary of a Young Girl*. In June 1944, Anne wrote her second-to-last diary entry:

> *Now I am getting really hopeful, now things are going well at last. Super news! An attempt has been made on Hitler's life and not even by Jewish communists or English capitalists this time, but by a proud German general. . . . It certainly shows that there are lots of officers and generals who are sick of the war and would like to see Hitler descend into a bottomless pit.*[3]

One night in 1958, a stage presentation in Linz of Anne's story was interrupted by youths. They claimed that the diary was a fake. A few days later, a teacher told Wiesenthal that half the students in his class had parents who had been active Nazis during the war. These children had been taught that the Holocaust was a hoax.

Wiesenthal decided that finding the Gestapo agent who had arrested the Franks would be his top priority. That way, he would be able to prove the diary was authentic and that the Holocaust had indeed occurred.

"I read the diary as a Jew, as a father of a girl the same age, and as an investigator in search of names," Wiesenthal later recalled.[4]

In a statement that Anne's father had written to accompany the diary, Wiesenthal found the name "Silberthaler." He was listed as the arresting officer. Wiesenthal knew that Austrians had been in charge of the Gestapo in the section of Amsterdam where the Franks hid. However, he did not think the name

"Silberthaler" looked Austrian. He decided to investigate people with that name or similar names. He ran into many dead ends.

Then, in May 1963, Wiesenthal learned that police in Amsterdam had a Nazi telephone list from the war years. He received a copy and examined it. Among the three hundred names was a Karl Silberbauer. Wiesenthal contacted the Austrian authorities. He explained his theory and asked them to investigate Silberbauer.

The following November, Karl Silberbauer, a

Simon Wiesenthal attended many trials of Nazi war criminals, like this one in Vienna in 1958. With the help of a network of volunteers, Wiesenthal brought more than one thousand Nazi war criminals to prosecution.

low-ranking inspector on the Austrian police force, was interviewed by the Austrians. When asked, Silberbauer admitted his guilt. "Yes, I arrested Anne Frank," he said.[5] He was temporarily suspended from the police force.

Later, when this exposure made international news, Silberbauer was asked by a reporter if he had read the diary. "Bought the little book last week to see if I'm in it," he said. "But I'm not."[6]

"Silberbauer is a zero," Wiesenthal said, explaining that he was not a powerful Nazi. "But the figure before the zero was Anne Frank and that raises his denomination."[7] Most important, Wiesenthal was able to prove the diary was real. So even though Silberbauer was only suspended, Wiesenthal believed the incident to be a great victory for Holocaust survivors.

During this time, Wiesenthal also developed a case on Karl Babor. He discovered that this Austrian doctor who took care of royalty in Ethiopia had been an SS officer at the Breslau concentration camp in Poland. Babor denied the charge but killed himself in January 1964.

In October 1966, sixteen SS officers were tried in Stuttgart, West Germany, for their participation in the killing of Jews in Lvov. Nine of the Nazis had been uncovered by Wiesenthal.

Wiesenthal also found a cruel camp guard named Anton Fehringer. All Wiesenthal originally knew about him was that Fehringer was from northern Austria. One day, Wiesenthal went to the library to check wartime newspapers for more clues. While he was there, he overheard two people discussing family trees. This gave

Wiesenthal an idea. He went home and contacted a genealogist he knew. Could this expert locate any towns in northern Austria where families named Fehringer lived? Within two days, the genealogist reported that he had located several Fehringer families in one particular town. One of Wiesenthal's helpers investigated them and found the wanted camp guard. He was later convicted of his crimes.

Perhaps Wiesenthal's most sensational case during this time was finding Franz Stangl. This Nazi had commanded the Treblinka extermination camp in Poland. There, at least four hundred thousand men, women, and children were killed. He also commanded Sobibor, another death camp. In all, Stangl was believed to be responsible for more than seven hundred thousand deaths. He had been arrested at the end of the war but escaped and then disappeared with his family.

Wiesenthal first learned of Stangl in 1948, when he saw the name on a list of deliveries from Treblinka to Berlin. These deliveries included hundreds of freight cars of clothing, wedding rings, even women's hair. These items obviously had been taken from doomed Jews and were being sent to Nazi headquarters.

Wiesenthal's file on Stangl quickly grew with information and reports from his many sources. He theorized that Stangl had moved to Syria in the early 1960s and then to Brazil.

Then one day in 1964, a former Gestapo agent visited Wiesenthal at his center. "I know where you can find Franz Stangl," he told Wiesenthal, "but it is going to cost you $25,000."[8]

Wiesenthal told the man that he did not have much money. The man began to bargain with him. "How many people did Stangl murder?" he asked.[9] About seven hundred thousand, Wiesenthal answered. "All right," said the visitor. "I'll give you a special price. How about a penny a head? That makes $7,000." Wiesenthal, trembling with rage, replied, "It's a deal."[10]

The man told Wiesenthal that Stangl lived in São Paulo, Brazil, and worked as a mechanic. It took Wiesenthal three more years to verify this information. "Secrecy was all important," he explained later. "Obtain the cooperation of Brazil, but limit knowledge of our plans to the smallest possible number of people. In the past, deliberate bureaucratic leaks had enabled men to escape."[11]

Finally, in 1967, Stangl was arrested as he returned home from his mechanic's job. "I knew I would be captured," he said later.[12] He was tried in Düsseldorf, West Germany, in 1970. Stangl was the highest-ranking death-camp official that West Germany had prosecuted. He received life imprisonment and later died in prison.

After the verdict, Wiesenthal walked out of the courtroom. He took out of his wallet a photo of Stangl that he kept as motivation. He tore it up and threw it away; he would not need it anymore. Wiesenthal later said that Stangl's sentencing "was purely symbolic. No punishment could be equated with the enormity of the crime. The important thing was that guilt had been established and justice done."[13]

Most of Wiesenthal's catches were men, since

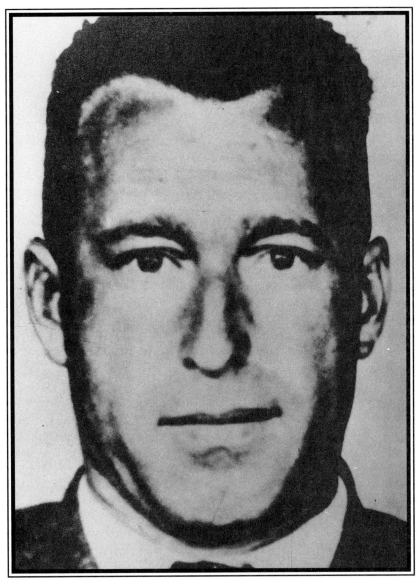

Franz Stangl, Nazi commander of the Treblinka death camp and the Sobibor death camp, was believed responsible for more than seven hundred thousand deaths. After Wiesenthal tracked him down in Brazil, Stangl was sentenced to life imprisonment.

women did not hold high-ranking jobs in the Nazi regime. One woman he did bring to justice was Hermine Braunsteiner. He first heard of her in April 1964. Wiesenthal was at a café in Tel Aviv, Israel. A woman recognized the now famous Nazi hunter and approached him. She told Wiesenthal that during World War II, she had been imprisoned at the Majdanek concentration camp in Poland. A female guard named Hermine Braunsteiner used a vicious dog and heavy whip to make female prisoners behave. "She must answer for her crimes," the woman told Wiesenthal.[14]

Wiesenthal began investigating. He learned that in 1949, Braunsteiner had been convicted of torturing female inmates at another concentration camp. She spent three years in prison for her crimes there. After her release, Braunsteiner lived in Austria and then Germany. There, she met an American construction worker. They were married and went to the United States to live. Braunsteiner became a naturalized citizen in 1963 and lived in Maspeth, New York.

As Wiesenthal was gathering this information, he received new statements about other crimes Braunsteiner had committed. Then he contacted the United States government. Several years of legal maneuvering followed.

Wiesenthal wrote his autobiography, *The Murderers Among Us*, in 1967. A book reviewer said it read like a "fascinating detective thriller" and added, "Sickening at times, it eventually provides the warm satisfaction of following a righteous job well done. You just can't lay the book down until it is finished."[15] Another reviewer wrote:

> For all the books and movies that plumb our grue-
> some fascination with Nazi villains, few writers
> capture the joy that comes from tracking them down.
> One of the few is Simon Wiesenthal. . . . There's . . .
> something unmistakably right when the losers and
> victims win, when the good guys stomp the bad, or
> at least put up a fight.[16]

During a visit to the United States to promote the book, Wiesenthal held a press conference to offer details on the Braunsteiner case. Finally, Braunsteiner was extradited to Germany in 1973. She received a sentence of life in prison. She was the first accused criminal to be deported from the United States to face trial in Germany.

Finding the wanted Nazis gave Wiesenthal a great deal of satisfaction. Just as important, however, was finding witnesses to their crimes. If no witnesses came forward, these men and women stood a good chance of being set free once they were caught.

One time, Wiesenthal found witnesses but decided against seeking prosecution. In his 1981 book, *Max and Helen*, Wiesenthal described the case. In the early 1960s, a passenger on a train told Wiesenthal about a concentration camp commander who had disappeared after the war. The man had become an executive in a big German company. This passenger was not a wit-ness, so Wiesenthal had to find people who had actual, firsthand knowledge of the man's crimes.

There were only two living witnesses to the

Wiesenthal refused to tolerate suggestions that the Holocaust was a hoax. By finding the Gestapo agent who had arrested Anne Frank and her family, Wiesenthal proved to all doubters that Anne Frank's diary was authentic.

commander's crimes. In his book, Wiesenthal called the witnesses Max and Helen. The couple had been engaged during the war and had been sent to the same concentration camp. Helen was raped by the commander. Shortly before the war ended, she gave birth to a baby boy. She told her son that his real father had been a Jew who had been killed fighting the Nazis. Her son grew to hate the Nazis.

Neither Max nor Helen wished to testify against the commander. They feared that Helen's son, called Marek in the book, would find out the identity of his real father. Max told Wiesenthal:

> *Simon, the dead that [the camp commander] has on his conscience can't be brought back to life by my testimony. But the living, Helen and Marek, could be ruined by it. It's a paradox, but their right to a peaceful life depends on criminals like [the commander] being allowed to go on living as free citizens.*[17]

Wiesenthal replied:

> *It would be the first time I have let a criminal go free against whom I have such clear-cut evidence. But . . . if [the commander] is to go free, it must depend on you and Helen only. You two shall decide. You are probably the only survivors of the camp he commanded. Believe me when I say I didn't leave a stone unturned to find other witnesses to his crimes. And failed.*[18]

Wiesenthal tore up all the information he had compiled. The camp commander went free, and Marek never learned his father's true identity.

9

Getting Away
With Murder

Thanks to Simon Wiesenthal, justice was served in more than one thousand cases of men and women who took part in Nazi war crimes. However, some who were responsible for the most heinous acts eluded Wiesenthal's grasp. Perhaps if Wiesenthal had had more financial and official support, he would have been able to track down the criminals quickly. Or maybe if Odessa had not been such a well-planned organization, these Nazis would not have escaped. Regardless, they continually haunted Wiesenthal during the decades after he reopened his documentation center.

One of the most frustrating of Wiesenthal's searches was for Dr. Josef Mengele. He was a barbaric

SS doctor who was known as the "Angel of Death." Mengele was responsible for selecting prisoners to be killed in the gas chambers at the Auschwitz and Birkenau concentration camps. There, about 2 million people died. In front of the Auschwitz crematorium Mengele was once heard to say, "Here the Jews enter through the door and leave through the chimney."[1]

Many of those whom Mengele spared from immediate death were subjected to cruel and extremely painful genetic experiments. Mengele often chose twins for his most bizarre procedures. Many of these torturous treatments were attempts to create a master race of blond-haired, blue-eyed people.

Toward the end of 1944, as the Soviet army neared Auschwitz, Mengele disappeared. He lived under his own name in Gunzberg, West Germany, where his prominent family owned a farm-equipment plant. During the war crimes trials in Nuremberg, Mengele's name was mentioned frequently.

In 1949, West German officials made moves to arrest Mengele. Before they could get to him, however, he escaped with the aid of Odessa. Wiesenthal, sifting through reports and clues provided by his network of helpers, learned that Mengele was living in Argentina. The Nazi hunter contacted authorities in West Germany and Israel. The Germans asked Argentine authorities to extradite Mengele, but they refused. Israel made plans to kidnap Mengele and bring him to Israel for prosecution. However, Mengele was able to get away in time.

Wiesenthal would not let the matter rest. "If I

could get this man, my soul would finally be at peace," Wiesenthal once said.[2]

Through his sleuthing, Wiesenthal concluded that Mengele entered Paraguay in May 1959 and was granted citizenship. Authorities in that country denied it, however. Wiesenthal said he had proof that Mengele was living in a German-owned villa among a community of other Germans. Mengele traveled with four armed guards, Wiesenthal said. Before Mengele entered any building, even the home of a German friend, two of his guards entered first to make sure it was safe. Then they signaled to the guards who had remained with Mengele.[3]

Despite these precautions, Wiesenthal said, Mengele was seen drinking at a German-owned bar in Paraguay. He wore dark glasses and occasionally waved a pistol about. The Nazi hunter also gathered proof that Mengele was an active member of The Spider. The members of this group of Nazi officials protected one another. They also were involved in extortion and smuggling in South America.

Other evidence indicated that Wiesenthal was incorrect in some of his assertions. During the period that the Nazi hunter believed the mad doctor was in Paraguay, some reports said that Mengele had moved to Brazil. By then he was in very poor health. Then a report surfaced that Mengele had drowned in Brazil.

Wiesenthal refused to believe this information because reports of Mengele's death had surfaced in the past. He was also continuing to receive many reports of Mengele sightings in Paraguay. Then, in 1985, Brazilian authorities provided bones for experts

Barbed wire topped the gates at Auschwitz, where Dr. Josef Mengele, nicknamed the "Angel of Death," performed his cruel human experiments. Millions of innocent people were killed in the gas chambers at this death camp.

to examine. These experts concluded that they were, indeed, the bones of Mengele. The mad doctor was dead, though his demise left many Jews with little sense of satisfaction.

During the search for Mengele, Wiesenthal was also searching for Martin Bormann, Hitler's chosen successor. Wiesenthal said he had proof that Bormann was in Brazil and was very well off. However, Wiesenthal could not persuade government authorities to bring the Nazi to justice. "No country will want to attempt a second Eichmann case," Wiesenthal complained in 1967. "Bormann will come to his end some day, and the West German reward of [twenty-five thousand dollars] will never be paid."[4]

Evidence turned up later that indicated Bormann may actually have killed himself in Berlin in May 1945, as the Allies took over Germany. The status of Bormann may forever remain a mystery.

As the years passed, Wiesenthal realized that the number of "clients" on his wanted list was dwindling. Those who had escaped punishment would soon face what Wiesenthal once called "the biological solution," that is, a natural death.[5] Nevertheless, Wiesenthal still had work to do.

Telling the World

By the mid-1970s, with the majority of the most-wanted Nazis either dead or captured, Wiesenthal's work as a supersleuth began to come to an end. Still, he was not content to sit back and retire. Instead, he spent more time writing and lecturing.

Wiesenthal served as a consultant to the 1974 feature film *The Odessa File.* He also worked to change statute-of-limitation laws. For example, both Austria and Germany had twenty-year limits on the prosecutions of war crimes. Wiesenthal wanted the United Nations to declare that genocide—the systematic killing of people of a particular national or ethnic group—was not restricted by statutes of limitations.

Another of Wiesenthal's projects was persuading the Canadian government to take action against supposed war criminals living in that country. He accused the Canadian government of allowing war criminals to come to Canada after the war, without fear of prosecution. Wiesenthal said he would refuse to travel to Canada until the government took action.

In 1980, Canada's solicitor-general, Robert Kaplan, met with Wiesenthal at the Canadian Embassy in Washington, D.C. He told the Nazi hunter that his country would set up a committee to explore legal ways to bring suspected war criminals to justice. Kaplan said that because these people were now Canadian citizens, they were under no legal obligation to disclose their past.[1]

Five years later, a Toronto newspaper published information confirming that eleven suspected war criminals were Canadian citizens. Yet nothing was being done to bring them to trial. "I am disappointed about the Canadians," Wiesenthal said. "I expected better."[2]

Sometimes Wiesenthal's outspokenness caused him to become involved in nasty public disputes. In November 1975, for example, Bruno Kreisky was elected chancellor of Austria. Shortly after the election, Wiesenthal called a press conference. He accused a major politician of having served in a World War II SS unit that killed ten thousand people in Eastern Europe. Kreisky, who had been planning to appoint this man to a prominent position in his government, was furious.[3] He called Wiesenthal a man "not too careful with the truth" and declared,

"These stories from long ago must finally come to an end."[4] Kreisky also insinuated that Wiesenthal had helped the Nazis during World War II.

Prominent people came to the Nazi hunter's defense. "As far as we know, Wiesenthal can document his clean record, while [the politician's] unclean past is notorious," said a top West German prosecutor of Nazi criminals.[5] "Wiesenthal has almost never been wrong," added one of Kreisky's former top aides, "and . . . Kreisky knows it."[6]

Wiesenthal also had public disputes with other Nazi hunters. One of these focused on the controversy surrounding Kurt Waldheim. Waldheim, an Austrian, was named secretary general of the United Nations in 1971. Shortly after that, rumors began surfacing about his Nazi past. Waldheim denied all the stories. Then, in 1986, he announced that he would run for the presidency of Austria.

Waldheim's military record became a huge public issue. Some Jews accused the secretary general of war crimes. Beate Klarsfeld took part in public protests against Waldheim. Klarsfeld and her husband, Serge, were famous Nazi hunters.

Serge Klarsfeld was a young Jewish boy living with his family in France when World War II broke out. His father was killed by the Nazis. After the war, Serge became a lawyer and married Beate, a German woman who was Protestant. Together, they dedicated their lives to pursuing Nazis.

Beate Klarsfeld first came to the public's attention in the late 1960s, when she discovered that German leader Kurt-Georg Kiesinger had worked for the notorious Nazi Joseph Goebbels during World War II. Beate publicized Kiesinger's role. She was credited with his defeat when he ran for reelection in 1969.

In the 1970s, the Klarsfelds exposed three former Gestapo leaders. Then, in the 1980s, they discovered where Nazi leader Klaus Barbie was hiding. Barbie had ordered more than four thousand executions during the Holocaust. He also had deported almost eight thousand Jews to the concentration camps. Nicknamed the "Butcher of Lyons," Barbie had what many of his survivors said was a great enthusiasm for torture and terror. The Klarsfelds campaigned relentlessly to get Barbie extradited from Bolivia and sent to France for trial. He was extradited in 1983.

The Klarsfelds admitted in 1985 that they supported assassinating war criminals if that was the only way to punish them for their war crimes. The only punishment Wiesenthal favored was what the courts handed out.[7]

Wiesenthal also disagreed with the Klarsfelds about Waldheim. Wiesenthal said he doubted the secretary general's claims of not knowing about war crimes in his military unit. However, the Nazi hunter had not seen enough proof that Waldheim had actually taken part in them. "He may be a liar and he may suffer from unforgivable lapses of memory," Wiesenthal said, "but that does not make him a war criminal."[8] He added, "I am fighting for the truth—the historic truth—without emotions."[9] Waldheim won the 1986 election, but in 1991 he decided against trying for a second term.

Wiesenthal also had disagreements with Elie

Wiesel, the novelist and war survivor who first used the term "Holocaust" to describe the mass murder of Jews by the Nazis. Wiesel, a Jew, was a child during the Holocaust. He survived his experience at the Auschwitz and Buchenwald concentration camps but lost his entire family. After the war, he went to live in France. He decided not to speak about his experiences until he could figure out the best way to do so.

About a decade later, Wiesel began pouring his emotions into writing. He authored about twenty novels, volumes of poetry, and other books about his experiences and those of other Jews. Wiesel became known as the "Poet of the Holocaust." He won a Nobel Prize for his work.

In 1978, President Jimmy Carter asked Wiesel to head the President's Commission on the Holocaust. Under Wiesel's leadership, the group recommended that a museum and study center be built. Today, the Holocaust Museum in Washington, D.C., serves as a memorial to those who died and tells the story of that horrible time to visitors from around the world.

Undoubtedly, the museum is a very important tool for remembering the Holocaust. Yet Wiesenthal hinted that some of its organizers were concerned only about the suffering of the Jews in the Holocaust, and that they ignored the other groups who were also persecuted by Hitler and the Nazis.

Wiesenthal supported Hitler's other victims, not just the Jews. In his book *Max and Helen,* Wiesenthal wrote:

> *The German war of vengeance was not directed only at the Jews, but against other nations too. But . . .*

the war against the Jews was easier to wage because the Nazis could depend on an anti-Semitism that had been deeply rooted for centuries.

Poland is an especially startling example. Incited by agents, anti-Semitic propaganda found support in certain sections of the population. . . . Even before the Germans fell upon the land, radicals of the right and anti-Semitic Poles had prepared the occupation troops for the persecution of Jews.[10]

Wiesenthal's work led not only to disagreements but also to danger. He continually received telephoned death threats. At one time, a branch of the World Union of National Socialists, a white-supremacist group based in Arlington, Virginia, offered a $40,000 reward for Wiesenthal's life.[11]

"Threats indicate to me that criminals at large know they are being sought," Wiesenthal once said. "I simply have a moral obligation to keep after these men. They must know that they are still held accountable, and none of them at this moment knows whether or not justice is just a step behind him."[12]

The Nazi hunter's office was vandalized, and in 1982, a bomb exploded at the front door of his house in Vienna. Much damage occurred, but fortunately, no one was injured. After that, armed policemen were stationed around-the-clock in front of Wiesenthal's house and office. He also had a peephole and a video surveillance system installed in his office. He began carrying a gun, yet remained fatalistic about his chances. "If I worried about being shot, I would not be able to live," he said. "When my time has come, it has come."[13]

In 1985, Wiesenthal spent twenty days lecturing at colleges and universities in the United States. "People had a hard time believing he has devoted his entire life to pursing these people," said a student at Indiana University in Bloomington. "How does someone live like this?"[14]

Indeed, it was emotionally difficult. Aside from stamp collecting and spending time with his grandchildren, Wiesenthal had few diversions in his life. In fact, in 1986, Cyla begged her husband to stop his work so that the couple could lead a normal life. "I cannot stop—I would feel like a traitor," he told her.

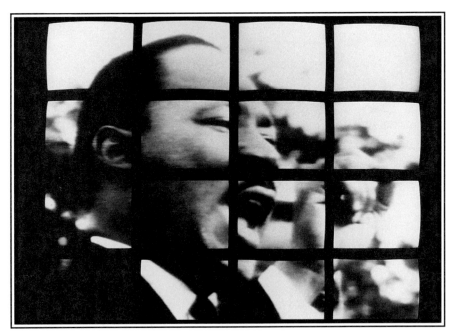

Simon Wiesenthal was also outspoken in supporting other minority groups targeted by Hitler and the Nazi party. The Museum of Tolerance displays this Martin Luther King, Jr., Civil Rights Wall.

Then he told an interviewer, "Sometimes she must feel, 'I am not married to a husband—I am married to millions of dead people.'"[15]

Even other Holocaust survivors wondered about his diligence. One time a Jewish man who had become a successful jeweler after the war asked Wiesenthal about his career choice. He noted that if Wiesenthal had resumed practicing architecture, he would have been very successful by now. Why did he not go back to designing houses?

Wiesenthal answered:

You're a religious man. You believe in God and life after death. I also believe. When we come to the other world and meet the millions of Jews who died in the camps and they ask us, "What have you done?" there will be many answers. You will say, "I became a jeweler." Another will say, "I smuggled coffee and American cigarettes." Another will say, "I built houses." But I will say, "I didn't forget you."[16]

Never Again

Simon Wiesenthal sees it clearly: He is back at the forced labor camp near the railyard, lined up with other prisoners. As the shooting begins, he is called away to paint a "Happy Birthday" poster for Adolf Hitler. Relieved to have been spared, he nonetheless cringes as he hears the screams of the others. "I think about those who did not survive," he said. "I feel guilty to be alive."[1]

This was not a nightmare but the filming of *Murderers Among Us*, a television movie based on Wiesenthal's 1967 autobiography. "Simon's story reminds you of the secret agents in fiction who get out of impossible predicaments with the help of their resourceful author," one of Wiesenthal's friends once said. "He has seen so many people killed that he inevitably asks himself why he was spared. He feels he owes an enormous debt that he can pay off only in symbolic installments."[2]

The 1988 movie starred Academy Award winner Ben Kingsley as Simon. The real Wiesenthal served as a consultant on the movie, which was filmed in Budapest. "I was transported back," Wiesenthal recalled. "It was so real. I was crying and crying."[3] He was not the only one. "The extras, the actors, everybody was crying," commented the movie's producer.[4]

Added Kingsley, "Simon is dynamite when he tells a story. He gets ambushed by waves of memory."[5] Kingsley also said that he was amazed by Wiesenthal's diligence in his work.

In 1989, a year after the television movie, Wiesenthal published his tenth book, *Justice Not Vengeance*. The eighty-year-old author, ailing with a heart condition, noted that it would probably be his final book. Aside from recounting his more famous cases, Wiesenthal made a plea to his younger readers. Remember. Remember. Remember that as awful as the Holocaust was, it could easily happen again, anytime, anywhere. He wrote:

> *You should . . . go into battle against the small injustices. Often this takes just as much civil courage and bravery as the struggle against the great wrongs. If a person looks the other way when his colleague at work is unjustly slandered, if he likes the idea of perhaps stepping into his position, then he is acting no differently from the person who looked the other way when the Jews were made to scrub the pavements,*

Wiesenthal stands in front of photographs at the Museum of Tolerance. He has devoted his life to the millions of victims of the Holocaust. "I didn't forget you," he says.

and who was happy to move into their abandoned homes.[6]

Wiesenthal has not trained anyone to take his place at the Jewish Documentation Center in Vienna. When the Nazi hunter dies, it may close. Through the Simon Wiesenthal Center in Los Angeles, however, his mission will endure. In 1996, for example, the center sent letters to hundreds of Internet-access providers and universities. The letters implored them to refuse to carry messages that "promote racism, anti-Semitism, mayhem and violence."[7]

The Internet's World Wide Web service allows users to publish electronic documents that can be read by millions of people. Many racist groups have used the web to publicize their views. Such "hate speech" is usually legal.

"Internet providers have a First Amendment right and a moral obligation not to provide these groups with a platform for their destructive propaganda," wrote Rabbi Abraham Cooper, associate dean of the center.[8]

Wiesenthal has received much recognition for his life's work. In 1980, President Jimmy Carter awarded him the United States Congressional Gold Medal in a White House ceremony. Wiesenthal also received the Great Medal of Merit from the president of the German Federal Republic in 1985, and the Knight of the Honorary Legion of France award in 1986. Countless other awards and honorary degrees from around the world attest to the universal respect and admiration he enjoys.

Yet Simon Wiesenthal has a simple explanation for why he did what he did. "Forgiveness is a personal matter," he once said. "You have the right to forgive what has been done to you personally. You do not have the right to forgive what has been done to others."[9]

He added, "I think I am one of the last witnesses [to the Holocaust]. And a last witness, before he leaves this world, has an obligation to speak out. My work for half a lifetime is to inform people. My work is a warning for the murderers of tomorrow."[10]

Chronology

1908—Simon Wiesenthal is born on December 31 in the town of Buchach, part of the Austria-Hungary Empire.

1914—Austrian Archduke Francis Ferdinand is assassinated; World War I begins.

1915—Hans Wiesenthal, Simon's father, dies on the battlefield.

1918—Germany and its allies are defeated.

1923—German politician Adolf Hitler forms a new political party, the National Socialist German Workers' party, or Nazis.

1925—Hitler's autobiography, *Mein Kampf* ("My Struggle"), is published, outlining his anti-Semitism and thirst for power; Simon's mother remarries and moves her family to Dolina, Austria-Hungary.

1928—Wiesenthal graduates from high school; denied admittance to Polytechnic Institute because of quotas on Jewish students, he enrolls at Technical University of Prague to study architecture and engineering.

1933—Hitler becomes chancellor of Germany; the first concentration camps are established.

1936—American track and field athlete Jesse Owens wins four gold medals at the Olympic Games in Germany; Wiesenthal marries classmate Cyla Muller.

1939—Germans and Soviets invade Poland, breaking their nonaggression pact; Britain and France declare war on Germany and the Soviet Union to begin World War II.

1941—Simon and Cyla Wiesenthal are ordered to report to the Janowska concentration camp near Lvov; the United States enters World War II after Japan bombs the American military base at Pearl Harbor, Hawaii.

1942—Cyla Wiesenthal escapes from a concentration camp with a false passport; Hitler begins the Final Solution.

1943—Wiesenthal experiences eight months of freedom after his own escape from a concentration camp.

1944—Wiesenthal is recaptured and returned to the Janowska concentration camp; Allied troops arrive in Normandy, France, in the "D-Day" invasion.

1945—Hitler commits suicide; Wiesenthal is freed as concentration camps are liberated; Germany unconditionally surrenders, ending the war in Europe; Wiesenthal begins working for the United States Army's War Crimes Unit; Japan surrenders, ending World War II; Simon Wiesenthal is reunited with his wife, Cyla.

1946—The Wiesenthals' daughter, Pauline Rosa, is born; Allied forces set up a court in Nuremberg, Germany, to prosecute Nazi officials for war crimes.

1947—Wiesenthal opens the Jewish Documentation Center in Linz, Austria, and tracks down Franz Murer; Anne Frank's diary is published.

1948—The Republic of Israel is proclaimed a homeland for Jews.

1950—North Korea invades South Korea; troops from the United States as well as other countries become involved in the conflict.

1953—Wiesenthal sends information about Adolf Eichmann's whereabouts to the World Jewish Congress in New York and the Israeli consulate in Vienna.

1954—Wiesenthal closes the Jewish Documentation Center.

1960—Wiesenthal receives word that Israelis captured Eichmann in Buenos Aires, Argentina.

1961—After a trial in Israel, Eichmann is hanged for war crimes; Wiesenthal reopens the Jewish Documentation Center in Vienna, Austria.

1963—Wiesenthal tracks down the police officer who arrested Anne Frank and her family.

1966—Sixteen Nazi officers are prosecuted for their participation in the World War II killings of Jews in Wiesenthal's hometown of Lvov.

1967—Tracks down Franz Stangl; Wiesenthal's autobiography, *The Murderers Among Us*, is published.

1973—American citizen Hermine Braunsteiner is extradited to Germany to face trial for war crimes.

1974—Wiesenthal serves as a consultant to the movie *The Odessa File.*

1976—Wiesenthal's book *The Sunflower* is published.

1977—Wiesenthal opens Museum of Tolerance in Los Angeles, California.

1980—Is awarded the United States Congressional Gold Medal by President Jimmy Carter.

1981—Publishes *Max and Helen.*

1985—Brazilian authorities provide bones that experts later identify as the remains of Nazi doctor Josef Mengele.

1988—A television movie based on Wiesenthal's autobiography is aired.

1989—Publishes *Justice Not Vengeance.*

Chapter Notes

Chapter 1

1. *The World Book Encyclopedia*, 1995 Edition, Vol. 1 (Chicago: World Book, Inc., 1995), p. 559.

2. *World Book*, Vol. II, p. 124.

3. "Simon Wiesenthal," press release provided by the Simon Wiesenthal Center in Los Angeles, California.

4. Simon Wiesenthal, *The Murderers Among Us* (New York: McGraw-Hill Book Company, 1967), p. 8.

5. Associated Press, "'Last Nazi' Due in Italy for Trial," *Richmond Times-Dispatch*, November 21, 1995, p. 5A.

6. Simon Wiesenthal, *Justice Not Vengeance* (New York: Grove Weidenfeld, 1989), pp. 351–352.

Chapter 2

1. Simon Wiesenthal, *The Murderers Among Us* (New York: McGraw-Hill Book Company, 1967), p. 23.

2. Alan Levy, *The Wiesenthal File* (Grand Rapids, Mich.: William B. Eerdmans Publishing Company, 1993), p. 23.

3. Edward F. Dolan, Jr., *Adolf Hitler: A Portrait in Tyranny* (New York: Dodd, Mead & Company, 1981), pp. 79–80.

4. Levy, p. 32.

Chapter 3

1. Alan Levy, *The Wiesenthal File* (Grand Rapids, Mich.: William B. Eerdmans Publishing Company, 1993), p. 37.

2. Charles Moritz, ed., "Simon Wiesenthal," *Current Biography* (New York: H.W. Wilson, 1975), p. 441.

3. Clyde Farnsworth, "Sleuth With 6 Million Clients," *New York Times Magazine*, February 2, 1964, p. 11.

4. Ibid.

5. Levy, p. 49.

6. Simon Wiesenthal, *The Sunflower* (New York: Schocken Books, 1976), p. 32.

7. Ibid., p. 57.

8. Levy, p. 54.

Chapter 4

1. Anne Frank, *The Diary of a Young Girl* (New York: Bantam Books, 1993), p. 245.

2. Maurice Isserman, *America at War: World War II* (New York: Facts on File, 1991), p. 32.

3. Simon Wiesenthal, "The Murderers Among Us, Conclusion," *Saturday Evening Post*, March 11, 1967, p. 53.

4. Ibid.

5. Ibid.

6. Ibid.

7. Alan Levy, *The Wiesenthal File* (Grand Rapids, Mich.: William B. Eerdmans Publishing Company, 1993), p. 65.

8. Isserman, p. 172.

Chapter 5

1. Simon Wiesenthal, *Justice Not Vengeance* (New York: Grove Weidenfeld, 1989), p. 13.

2. Ibid., p. 30.

3. Clyde Farnsworth, "Sleuth With 6 Million Clients," *The New York Times Magazine*, February 2, 1964, p. 11.

4. Ann Walmsley, "Stalking the Nazis," *Maclean's*, December 9, 1985, p. 6.

5. Alan Levy, *The Wiesenthal File* (Grand Rapids, Mich.: William B. Eerdmans Publishing Company, 1993), p. 77.

Chapter 6

1. Ronald Gray, *Hitler and the Germans* (Minneapolis: Lerner Publications Company, 1983), p. 30.

2. Alan Levy, *The Wiesenthal File* (Grand Rapids, Mich.: William B. Eerdmans Publishing Company, 1993), p. 80.

3. Joseph P. Blank, "The Man Who Will Not Forget," *Reader's Digest*, February 1973, p. 156.

4. Ibid.

5. Simon Wiesenthal, *Max and Helen* (New York: William Morrow and Company, 1982), pp. 35–36.

6. Ibid., p. 77.

Chapter 7

1. Simon Wiesenthal, "The Murderers Among Us, Part I," *Saturday Evening Post*, February 25, 1967, p. 54.

2. Joseph P. Blank, "The Man Who Will Not Forget," *Reader's Digest*, February 1973, p. 156.

3. Ibid.

4. Ibid., p. 159.

5. Ibid.

6. Ibid., p. 160.

7. Clyde Farnsworth, "Sleuth With 6 Million Clients," *New York Times Magazine*, February 2, 1964, p. 46.

8. Gloria Emerson, "The Hunter," *Vogue*, June 1983, p. 208.

9. Ibid.

10. Malcolm Gray, "A Career of Nazi Hunting," *Maclean's*, May 25, 1987, p. 40.

Chapter 8

1. Ann Walmsley, "Stalking the Nazis," *Maclean's,* December 9, 1985, p. 7.

2. Clyde Farnsworth, "Sleuth With 6 Million Clients," *New York Times Magazine,* February 2, 1964, p. 11.

3. Anne Frank, *The Diary of a Young Girl* (New York: Bantam Books, 1993), p. 264.

4. Farnsworth, p. 46.

5. Ibid., p. 47.

6. "Intercontinental Op," *Time,* March 31, 1967, p. E3.

7. Farnsworth, p. 47.

8. "War Crimes," *Time,* March 10, 1967, p. 40.

9. Ibid.

10. Ibid.

11. Joseph P. Blank, "The Man Who Will Not Forget," *Reader's Digest,* February 1973, p. 164.

12. "War Crimes," p. 40.

13. Blank, p. 155.

14. Ibid., p. 160.

15. "The Hunters Become the Hunted," *Saturday Review,* April 15, 1967, p. 32.

16. Steve Weissman, "The Chase," *Harper's Magazine,* January 1975, p. 92.

17. Simon Wiesenthal, *Max and Helen* (New York: William Morrow and Company, 1982), p. 132.

18. Ibid., p. 133.

Chapter 9

1. Alan Levy, *The Wiesenthal File* (Grand Rapids, Mich.: William B. Eerdmans Publishing Company, 1993), p. 198.

2. "Wiesenthal's Last Hunt," *Time*, September 26, 1977, p. 36.

3. Ibid.

4. "Intercontinental Op," *Time*, March 31, 1967, p. 4E.

5. "Wiesenthal's Last Hunt," p. 38.

Chapter 10

1. Bogdan Kipling, "The Nazi-hunter Finds a New Ear," *Maclean's*, May 5, 1980, p. 36.

2. Ann Walmsley, "Stalking the Nazis," *Maclean's*, December 9, 1985, p. 7.

3. Fay Willey, "Digging Up the Past," *Newsweek*, December 1, 1975, p. 58.

4. Ibid.

5. Ibid.

6. Ibid.

7. Malcolm Gray, "A Career of Nazi Hunting," *Maclean's*, May 25, 1987, p. 40.

8. Ibid.

9. Ibid.

10. Simon Wiesenthal, *Max and Helen* (New York: William Morrow and Company, 1982), p. 70.

11. Walmsley, p. 7.

12. Joseph P. Blank, "The Man Who Will Not Forget," *Reader's Digest*, February 1973, p. 164.

13. Walmsley, p. 7.

14. Ibid., p. 6.

15. Ibid., p. 7.

16. Clyde A. Farnsworth, "Sleuth With 6 Million Clients," *New York Times Magazine*, February 2, 1964, p. 47.

Chapter 11

1. Jack Friedman, "On Location in Budapest, Nazi Hunter Simon Wiesenthal Relives the Horrors of His Past," *People*, August 1, 1988, p. 49.

2. Simon Wiesenthal, "The Murderers Among Us, Part I," *Saturday Evening Post*, February 25, 1967, p. 43.

3. Friedman, p. 49.

4. Ibid.

5. Ibid.

6. Simon Wiesenthal, *Justice Not Vengeance* (New York: Grove Weidenfeld, 1989), p. 359.

7. Peter H. Lewis, "Internet Ban on Hate Messages Urged," *Richmond Times-Dispatch*, January 11, 1996, p. 2A.

8. Ibid.

9. Ann Walmsley, "Stalking the Nazis," *Maclean's*, December 9, 1985, p. 7.

10. Friedman, p. 49.

Further Reading

Dolan, Edward F., Jr. *Adolf Hitler: A Portrait in Tyranny.* New York: Dodd, Mead & Company, 1981.

Frank, Anne. *The Diary of a Young Girl.* New York: Bantam Books, 1993.

Gray, Ronald. *Hitler and the Germans.* Minneapolis: Lerner Publications Company, 1983.

Isserman, Maurice. *America at War: World War II.* New York: Facts on File, 1991.

Levy, Alan. *The Wiesenthal File.* Grand Rapids, Mich.: William B. Eerdmans Publishing Company, 1993.

The Simon Wiesenthal Center, 9760 W. Pico Blvd., Los Angeles, Ca. 90035. Internet address: http://www.wiesenthal.com.

Wiesenthal, Simon. *The Murderers Among Us.* New York: McGraw-Hill Book Company, 1967.

———. *The Sunflower.* New York: Schocken Books, 1976.

———. *Max and Helen.* New York: William Morrow and Company, 1982.

———. *Justice Not Vengeance.* New York: Grove Weidenfeld, 1989.

Index